D0461078

Living on the Edge

Hot Deserts

WENDY PFEFFER

BENCHMARK BOOKS

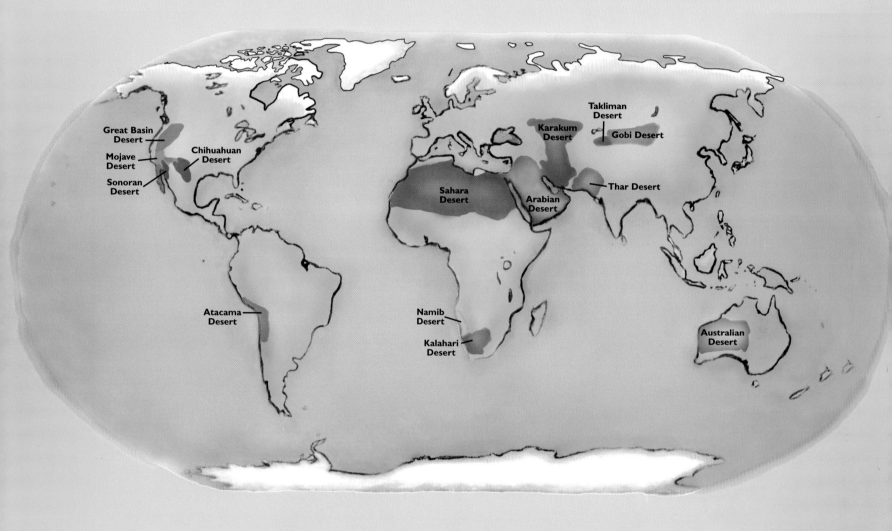

Great Basin
Desert

Mojave
Desert

Sonoran
Desert

Chihuahuan
Desert

Atacama
Desert

Sahara
Desert

Karakum
Desert

Takliman
Desert

Gobi Desert

Thar Desert

Arabian
Desert

Namib
Desert

Kalahari
Desert

Australian
Desert

Deserts of the World

Contents

A camel stands on the crackled ground of a dried up lake bed.

What Are Deserts?

Deserts are the driest places on Earth. Some, like the Sahara Desert in Africa, are hot. Others, like the Gobi Desert in Asia, are cold. But all deserts are dry. Deserts generally get fewer than 10 inches (25 centimeters) of rain a year. Several years may pass before the Atacama Desert in South America receives rain. Yet a flash flood can rip through even the driest desert and overflow ditches and empty streambeds. Hot sun and strong winds may then evaporate the floodwater, making the land bone-dry again.

During the day in many hot deserts, temperatures soar. Rocks and sand might reach 165 degrees Fahrenheit (74 degrees Celsius). At night, temperatures can dip to 40 degrees Fahrenheit (4°C). The next day sweltering hot winds blow across the sand dunes again. How can anything survive?

The Namib Desert is home to some of the world's highest sand dunes.

Saguaro cactus flowers

The Sahara looks like a lifeless expanse of sand, salt, rocks, and pebbles. But camels thrive there. In the Sonoran Desert, located in parts of California, Arizona, and Mexico, spring flowers carpet the sand and tree-sized cacti tower above them. Lizards, mice, scorpions, rattlesnakes, tortoises, kangaroo rats, and honeypot ants are just a few of the animals living on the Sonoran sand. The Namib Desert, along Africa's west coast, has fewer plants and less rain than the Sonoran.

Desert plants and animals live in the world's driest habitats. They have adapted by different means in order to survive. Many plants have long root systems that suck up rainwater to store in their leaves or

6

**A desert tortoise and a prickly pear cactus
in the Sonoran Desert**

stems. Waxy leaves keep the moisture from escaping. Desert life protects itself
from the heat and cold, and communities form in which plants and animals
help each other to survive.

Camels in Africa and Asia

A group of hot deserts stretches across North Africa, the Middle East, north-western India, and southeastern Pakistan. The largest, the Sahara Desert, is almost as big as the United States. Shifting sand dunes sprawl mile after mile under the searing sun.

One-humped Arabian camels thrive in these parched conditions. The Arabian camel's thick woolly hair shields its skin and insulates its body from brutally hot days and cold nights.

A camel can travel for two weeks or longer without drinking water. Pack camels move along at 25 miles (40 kilometers) a day, carrying loads of up to 400 pounds (182 kilograms). It's no wonder they are called "ships of the desert."

A camel caravan crossing the Sahara.

A one-humped camel

Imagine walking day after day in blistering heat without drinking, lugging a heavy load. Desert travel makes camels very thirsty. A camel can drink 30 gallons (114 liters) of water in ten minutes, causing its belly to bulge. Its sense

of smell is so good it can smell water several miles away.

A camel has a special way of saving body moisture. It does not sweat, unless the temperature soars. A camel also holds moisture in its nose. A lining in the nose sponges any wetness from the camel's breath before it exhales.

A long neck lets a camel hold its head up high to see far-off plant life, such as a date palm tree in an oasis. Strong teeth and jaws help the camel eat tough desert plants, its main diet. Sharp teeth in the front of its mouth cut and tear leaves and twigs. The camel chews with its flat back teeth, just like people do.

A camel's nose and neck are
well adapted to desert life.

Camels eat some desert plants that have spike-like thorns. The inside of a camel's mouth is lined with tough skin to protect it. Plants are rare on African deserts so a split upper lip allows camels to munch on short grasses close to the ground. When food is plentiful they store it as fat in their humps. When food is scarce, they live off of the fat.

Tough calluses on its chest and knees protect a camel's body from the hot sand when it kneels. Wide leathery pads

A camel munching on a desert plant.

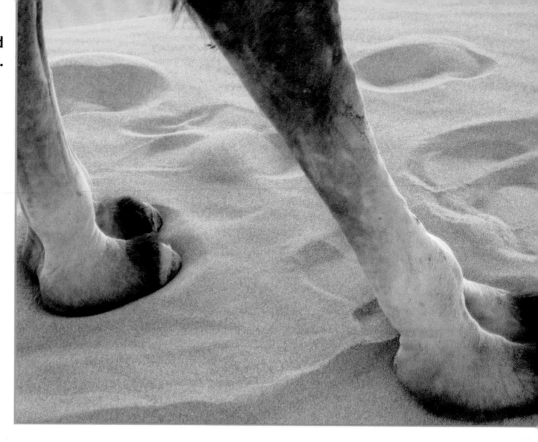

on the bottom of the camel's feet keep it from slipping. These pads connect the toes. When spread out, they keep the camel from sinking in the loose, shifting sand.

Because a camel's eyes are placed on the sides of its head, it can see in almost all directions. Thick eyebrows provide shade from the bright sun. Long, thick eyelashes protect the camel's eyes from the sun and blowing sand.

A clear eyelid comes up from below to cover each eye during a sandstorm. This eyelid is in addition to the camel's upper eyelid that blocks out light. Even though the camel cannot see as well through its clear eyelids as with its eyes open, it can see enough to know where it's going.

Another protection from sun and sand is thick hair growing in and around the camel's ears. Special muscles in a camel's nose let the camel squeeze its nostrils into narrow slits to keep out blowing sand. In a sandstorm a camel falls to its knees, squeezes its nostrils, and stays still until the storm is over. This practice saves the camel and the rider as well.

Baby camels are born in the spring and are hardy like their parents. They can walk the day they're born. Each calf is stiff-legged, goose-necked, and hump-backed, like its parents. Thanks to these adaptations, a camel might survive in the desert's hostile environment for 40 years.

A camel's long eyelashes and hairy ears protect it from blowing sand.

A camel and its baby

The Namib Desert has very few hiding places.

Survival in the Namib

The Sahara may be the largest desert in the world, but the Namib is the most unusual. It lies along the west coast of southern Africa. Blowing winds create sand dunes a thousand feet (305 meters) high. That's almost as high as the Empire State Building. Since there are few places to hide from predators most animals have reddish coloring that camouflages them. They blend with the reddish sand of the Namib.

The Namib Desert is near the ocean, but years go by without rain. Rain clouds almost never form over the cold water near the Namib. But sometimes fog forms and drifts inland. Fog develops when cold ocean currents cool the warm air over the desert. Desert animals gather this small amount of moisture and use it to survive.

One beetle puts its head near the ground and its belly up in the air. When the fog rolls in, the condensed water

Fog drifts over the Namib.

A "fog-basking" beetle takes advantage of a fog cloud

on its belly rolls down to its mouth. A sand grouse adapts to the drought in a different way. It flies great distances across the desert to a water hole. It soaks its breast feathers and carries this water back to the young in its nest.

The sidewinder viper collects moisture by licking morning dew off its body before the sun evaporates it. Imagine if the only water a person had were a few drops each morning! The viper also lifts different parts of its body at different times. None of it stays on the blistering hot sand for more than a moment. While slip-sliding across the desert the viper leaves tracks that look like the rungs of a ladder. When it stops, it burrows quickly, then peers out to look for lizards. With eyes near the top of its head, it can easily spot one. The viper quickly strikes its prey and kills it with a poisonous bite.

To hide itself from predators, a dancing white lady spider weaves sand into its sticky web over the entrance of its burrow. This

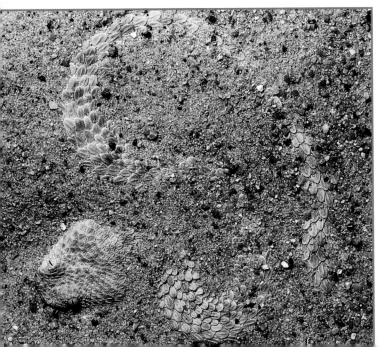

A Namib viper awaits its prey

18

A dancing white lady spider

camouflages the entrance. If the spider is threatened, it dances on its long legs to frighten off an enemy, such as a wasp. The wheel spider escapes by turning its body into a ball. It folds up its legs and cartwheels down a sandy slope. With dunes a thousand feet high, it may be a long way to the bottom.

An organ pipe cactus in the Sonoran Desert

Life in the Sonoran Desert

On the harsh, dry Sonoran Desert millions of wildflowers appear in the spring. Saguaro cactus, prickly pear cactus, and many other species of these tough drought-resistant plants thrive there too. Roots soak up rainwater during the infrequent winter and summer rains. The cactus stores the water in its trunk to use during the dry times.

After a rainstorm a saguaro can draw up to 200 gallons (760 liters) of water into its pleated trunk, enough water to fill a bathtub three times. The trunk swells and shrinks depending on how much water it's holding.

When it is full of water, a saguaro can live through months of drought.

A saguaro cactus can grow 50 feet (15 meters) tall, as high as a five-story building, and weigh 6 tons, about as much as a full-grown elephant. Inside a saguaro cactus it is 10 degrees cooler than outside. Many different kinds of animals, including lizards, seek shelter inside cactus trunks. Many desert animals use cacti to help them survive.

Some animals eat the pulpy saguaro cactus fruits that have fallen to the ground. Others eat its seeds. Birds and bats sip its nectar. Owls and hawks perch on it. Woodpeckers peck holes in its fingerlike trunk and raise their babies in them. The young birds are out of the hot sun during the day and insulated from the cold at night. Elf owls use the woodpeckers' abandoned nests.

A nest of red-tailed hawk chicks high up on a saguaro cactus

A long-nosed bat sipping nectar from a saguaro flower.

A long-nosed bat eating saguaro fruit.

A fringe-toed lizard uses its wedge-shaped head to burrow under the sand.

Buried in sand, a fringe-toed lizard is almost invisible.

Many animals move out of the hot sun into the saguaro's safe haven. They are protected from predators that can't climb the cactus's steep thorny trunk. A large cactus is like an apartment house with many different tenants.

Fringe-toed lizards are well named, since they have fringes of flat scales on their hind feet. These fringes grip the sand, letting the lizard run quickly over the desert to catch insects. And they help it wiggle under the sand when predators are near. It digs in with its wedge-shaped head, kicks with its fringed feet, slips in the sand with its smooth body, and disappears in seconds.

Fringed-toed lizards "swim" a short distance in loose sand to fool predators. Under the sand the lizard can close its ears with flaps of skin and squeeze its nostrils shut, just as a camel does. It also has a pair of clear eyelids, like a camel, to protect its eyes. The lizard's lower jaw fits tightly into its upper jaw to keep sand out of its mouth. Its light-colored body blends with the sand and camouflages the lizard to protect it from birds hovering overhead and predators on the sand.

A desert tortoise rarely drinks but gets moisture from eating fruits, grasses, and wildflowers. Desert tortoises eat so many prickly pear cactus fruits, the juice stains their faces purple. They store water in their bladder and can survive months of drought.

A desert tortoise eating wildflowers.

Other Animals Adapt and Survive

Hot parched deserts hold many surprises. At night when the desert cools, it comes alive. Birds sing. Rodents scurry. Spiders search for insects. And long-nosed bats sip sweet nectar from century plant blossoms. The plant's nectar provides energy for the bats. In return the bats help the plant survive by carrying pollen from one flower to another.

Deserts are remarkable habitats. They are not sandy wastelands, but homes for communities of living things that exist together. Many plants and animals have learned to adapt to heat and drought and sudden downpours and have survived. They have adapted so well to living in hot dry deserts that they might not be able to survive anywhere else on Earth.

A herd of camels gathers near a watering hole.

They Survive Heat.

1. Mice burrow in the sand.

2. Scorpions take shelter under stones.

3. Some lizards run on their hind legs to keep their bodies and front feet off the sizzling sand.

4. Kangaroo rats keep cool by sleeping under the sand.

They Survive Drought.

1. Hard, waterproof bodies keep beetles from drying out.

2. Web-footed geckos get moisture from the bodies of their prey.

3. Addax antelopes get moisture by eating plants that sprout after a rain.

4. Kangaroo rats get water from seeds they eat.

A kangaroo rat eating a piece of bark.

A shovel-snouted lizard dancing on hot sand.

A storage pot ant

They Find Food.

1. Pocket mice sleep when there's not enough food, and then wake up when there's plenty.

2. When nectar from desert flowers is plentiful, honeypot ants collect more than they can use. Some of the ants attach themselves to the roof of the colony and become living storage pots. The other ants feed nectar to the storage pot ants. Their bodies swell to grape-size. When nectar is scarce, the ants drink from the "storage pots."

3. Thorny devil lizards have been known to eat seven thousand ants a day, snatching them up with their sticky tongues. The lizard gets moisture from the ants' bodies.

THEY ESCAPE PREDATORS.

1. A chuckwalla fills its lungs with air when an enemy tries to pull it out of its hole.

2. When a hawk seizes the tail of a zebra-tailed lizard the tail falls off, setting the lizard free.

3. When a sand-diving lizard sees a predator approaching, it digs with its shovel-like snout and dives headfirst into the sand.

4. A horned lizard has sharp spines sticking out from its head and body to protect it from ene-mies. When disturbed, the horned lizard squirts jets of blood from its eyes.

5. Large thorns on a thorny devil lizard's head protect it against snakes that swallow their prey headfirst. Facing a head full of thorns may make a snake change its diet.

A spadefoot toad awakens.

THEY REPRODUCE.

1. Mosquitoes reproduce in the desert by using cavities in a cactus where rain-water collects. In the puddles their young can begin to grow.

2. Some fairy shrimp in the desert lay eggs that can survive twenty years in a dry lake bed. They hatch only when it rains.

3. The spadefoot toad sleeps underground for ten months. When it feels the vibrations of rain beating down, it comes out, eats, finds a pool of rainwater, and mates with another newly awakened spadefoot toad. The females lay eggs in the pool. Young toads develop, then bury themselves and wait for next year's rain.

GLOSSARY

ADAPT   to adjust to one's surroundings

COMMUNITY   a group of plants and animals that live together and interact with each other

CAMOUFLAGE   coloring or body shape that makes an animal hard to see in its natural surroundings

CONDENSE   to change from a gas to a liquid as when water vapor strikes a cool surface and makes it wet

DESERT   a geographic area that generally gets fewer than 10 inches (25 cm) of rain a year

DEW   water from the air that forms in little drops on cool surfaces at night

DROUGHT   a long time without rain

HABITAT   the place where an animal or plant is normally found

INSULATE   to cover something with a material that keeps heat in or out

OASIS   a fertile place with water in the desert

PREDATOR   an animal that catches and eats other animals

PREY   an animal hunted for food by another animal

FIND OUT MORE

Books

Guiberson, Brenda Z. *Cactus Hotel*. New York: Henry Holt, 1991.

Pringle, Laurence. *The Gentle Desert: Exploring an Ecosystem*. New York: Macmillan, 1977.

Sayre, April Pulley. *Desert*. New York: Twenty-First Century Books, 1994.

Spencer, Guy J. *A Living Desert*. Mahwah, NJ: Troll Associates, 1988.

Twist, Clint. *Ecology Watch: Deserts*. New York: Dillon Press, 1991.

Wiewandt, Thomas. *The Hidden Life of the Desert*. New York: Crown Publishers, 1990.

Wright-Frierson, Virginia. *A Desert Scrapbook: Dawn to Dusk in the Sonoran Desert*. New York: Simon and Schuster Books for Young Readers, 1996.

Web Site

Http://mbgnet.mobot.org/sets/desert/index.htm

INDEX

Page numbers in **boldface** are illustrations.

ABOUT THE AUTHOR

Wendy Pfeffer, an award-winning author of fiction and nonfiction books, enjoyed an early career as a first grade teacher. Now a full-time writer, she visits schools, where she makes presentations and conducts writing workshops. she lives in Pennington, New Jersey, with her husband, Tom.

For Steve, Bernadette, Andrew, and Sergio, always caring and supportive

With thanks to Kate Nunn for her patience in making sure every word was just right

With thanks to Dr. Dan Wharton, director of the Central Park Wildlife Center, Wildlife Conservation Society, for his expert review of this manuscript.

Benchmark Books
Marshall Cavendish
99 White Plains Road
Tarrytown, New York 10591-9001

www.marshallcavendish.com

Text copyright © 2003 Wendy Pfeffer
Map by Sonia Chaghatzbanian
Map copyright © 2003 Marshall Cavendish Corporation

Library of Congress Cataloging-in-Publication Data

Pfeffer, Wendy, 1929-
Hot deserts / by Wendy Pfeffer.
p. cm. — (Living on the edge)
Summary: Looks at the various kinds of plants and animals, including
camels, cactuses, and snakes, that survive in desert ecosystems
throughout the world.
Includes bibliographical references (p.   ) and index.
ISBN 0-7614-1440-1
1. Desert ecology—Juvenile literature.

Cover Photo: Corbis / Kevin Schafer

The photographs in this book are used by permission and through the courtesy of: *Animals Animals/ Earth Scenes*: Michael Fogden, 1, 17
(bottom), 19, 31; Turner, S. OSF, 5; Paul Jenkin, 15; Nigel Dennis, 16; Doug Wechsler, 20; Joe McDonald, 21 (top); Paddy Ryan, 34-35.
Corbis: Chase Swift, 4; Tann Arthus-Bertrand, 8; Shai Ginott, 9; Dave Bartruff, 10-11; Gallo Images, 12 (top); Bernard & Catherine Desjeux, 12 (bottom); Keren Su,
13; Craig Aurness, 14; Michael & Patricia Fogden, 17 (top), 18 (top); Kevin Fleming, 29; David A. Northcott, 36. *Photo Researchers*: C.K. Lorenz, 6, 7,
21 (bottom); Gregory G. Dimijian, 18 (bottom); Merlin D. Tuttle, Bat Conservation International, 22, 23; Tom McHugh, 24, 25, 30; Jerry L. Ferrara, 27;
Jacana, J. Phillipe, 32-33; Nigel J. Dennis, back cover.

Printed in Hong Kong

1 3 5 6 4 2